The Monsters Go on a Picnic

Colin and Jacqui Hawkins

PICTURE CORGI

Everyone is asleep and all is quiet in the monsters' house . . .

But not for long. brring! brring! brring! goes the alarm clock.

Mummy monster gets up and makes a pot of tea.

Meanwhile, Daddy monster is doing his exercises.

Splish! Splosh! All the little monsters are in the bathroom. What a mess.

Then Daddy monster comes in to clip his face hair.

Scrunch! Munch! Crunch!
It's monster breakfast time.

'Eat up, so you'll grow into big monsters,' says Daddy.

'It's a lovely day. Let's have a monster picnic,' decides Mummy monster.

They all run to the monster mobile.

Honk! Honk! Off they go. Soon they had left the town.

They were driving past green fields and could see sheep and cows.

The monsters can't wait to eat their delicious picnic.

They all gobble their peanut butter and jelly sandwiches and drink their monster fizz.

After lunch the little monsters go to see the animals.

They feed the chickens and geese and say hello to the cows.

All the monsters love the little foal.
Max monster gives her an apple.

They want to take her home with them.
Isn't she sweet?

It's time to go now. All the monsters have had a lovely day.

But where is Baby monster hiding?

Home again, the little monsters are all tired and muddy. 'Into the bath,' says Mummy.

Afterwards, warm and snug, they all drink their monster milk while Daddy reads a story.

THE MONSTERS GO ON A PICNIC
A PICTURE CORGI 0 552 523526
First published in 1984 by Beanstalk Books Ltd.
PRINTING HISTORY
Beanstalk Books publication 1984
Picture Corgi edition published 1986

Picture Corgi Books are published by
Transworld Publishers Ltd., 61-63 Uxbridge Road, Ealing
London W5 5SA
Printed by Purnell & Sons (Book Production) Ltd.